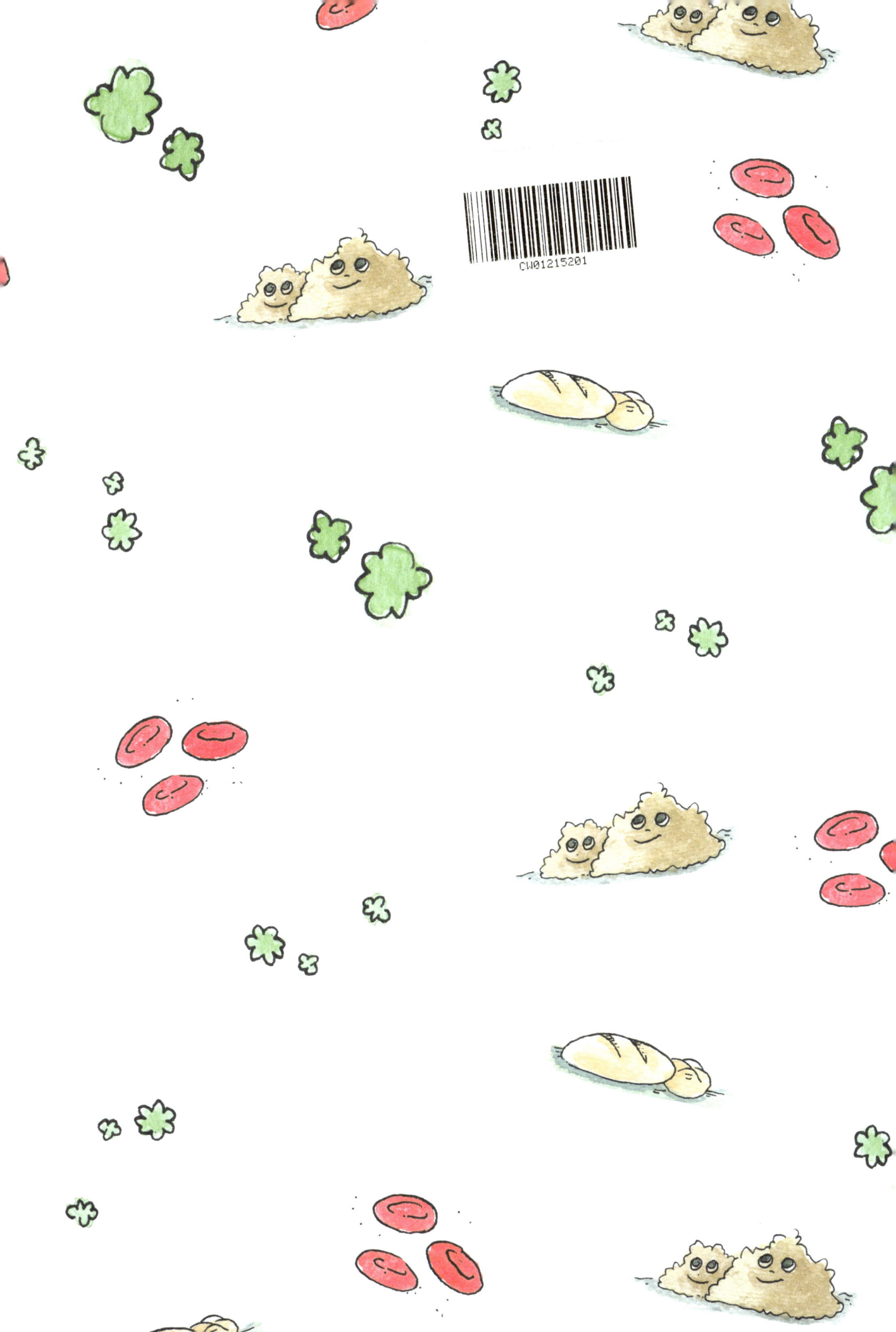

"This is dedicated to my children Rebecca, Rachael and Charlotte. Thanks to their precious presence in my life I have always had to keep an open and enquiring mind!"

© First published by Heather Hawley 2014.
Revised issue published in 2016.

All rights reserved. No part of this publication may be reproduced or transmitted in any form or by any means, electronic or mechanical, including photocopy, recording or any information storage and retrieval system without permission in writing from the author.

Copyright belongs to Heather Hawley.
The Busy Body Series 2016.

© Illustration and Design by Sarah-Leigh Wills.
www.happydesigner.co.uk

© BERTIE BREAD AND ROSIE - 2016
ISBN: 978-0-9931014-0-3

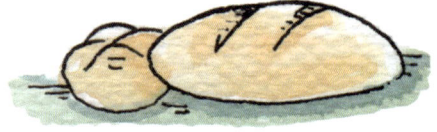

BERTIE BREAD AND ROSIE

Written by Heather Hawley
Illustrated by Sarah-Leigh Wills

CHAPTER 1

At the... Supermarket...

Bertie is a loaf of wholemeal bread. He is sitting on the top shelf at a local supermarket, having been there since the early hours of the morning.

He was made from wholemeal flour, milk, yeast, sugar and salt in a large, hot, noisy bakery just at the back of the supermarket. Now sitting big and proud on the shelf he is hoping that some happy person will take him back to a warm home where he can fill the tummies of some hungry people.

Quite a few people come to look at the bread shelves. A thin elderly man picks up Bertie and gives him a squeeze and a prod. 'Oh, careful!' thinks Bertie. He did not enjoy this but then thinks that if the man bought him, how happy the fellow might feel with a tummy full of Bertie Bread. However, the old man throws Bertie back on the shelf and takes a smaller loaf. Poor Bertie, he feels really rejected.

Eventually a little girl runs up to the bread shelf and says 'Please can I choose the bread today Mummy?' 'OK Rosie,' agrees her Mum.

Rosie is a very happy little girl with a big smile and pink cheeks. She is busy looking on the bottom shelf for bread. This makes Bertie really sad. 'I have no chance of being chosen by Rosie. She is so small she might not even realise I am here on the top shelf.'

Rosie is busy picking up loaves and putting them back. Then, she looks towards the top shelves, and to her delight she sees Bertie, a big brown loaf, just waiting to be made up into lovely chunky slices. Rosie's tummy rumbles: she is starting to feel quite hungry! Beaming she says: 'Mum, can we have that loaf off the top shelf?'

By this time Bertie decides he will not get chosen by Rosie and is looking to see who else in the shop might buy him. So when Rosie's Mum whisks Bertie off the shelf he has quite a shock!

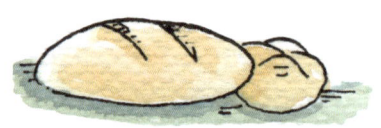

Bertie is placed in Rosie's shopping basket. Things are thrown in around him, until they get to the till. Then he is placed in a bag and Bertie sees nothing more until he is taken out and placed on Rosie's kitchen table.

'It's lovely here,' thinks Bertie.
The kitchen is a bright, warm place with
pots, pans and ornaments cluttering
the shelves and cupboards.

It is lunchtime and Rosie exclaims: 'my tummy is really rumbling Mummy! Can I have a slice of that lovely fresh bread please?' Hearing this Bertie gets very excited! Mum cuts a thick slice of Bertie and gives it to Rosie. 'Mmmm, thanks Mum,' she says, then curls up on a comfy chair and takes a big bite of Bertie… and this is where his adventure really begins…

CHAPTER 2
The Yellow Pool...

Bertie finds himself in Rosie's mouth, a big pink cave, edged with white boulders, which are Rosie's teeth. A large, wobbly muscular tongue and the teeth mix Bertie up with some clear liquid called saliva. This liquid helps to break him up into nice small bits. Suddenly, with a WHOOOOSH, he is skimming down a soft pink slide! This slide is quite short and is in two parts. The first bit has a funny name – the pharynx. Bertie is not in the pharynx for more than seconds before he finds himself in the second part – the oesophagus. With a quick squeeze from the oesophagus Bertie lands with a big splash into a sac that contains a lovely warm pool of yellow liquid known as gastric juices. This sac is known as a stomach and is inside Rosie's tummy. More and more bits of bread shoot down the pharynx then the oesophagus before being squeezed into Rosie's stomach. With a 'splish-splash' they join Bertie, swimming and playing around in the lovely yellow pool. Rosie doesn't feel hungry anymore with yummy bread in her tummy. Cosy and full, she falls asleep in the chair.

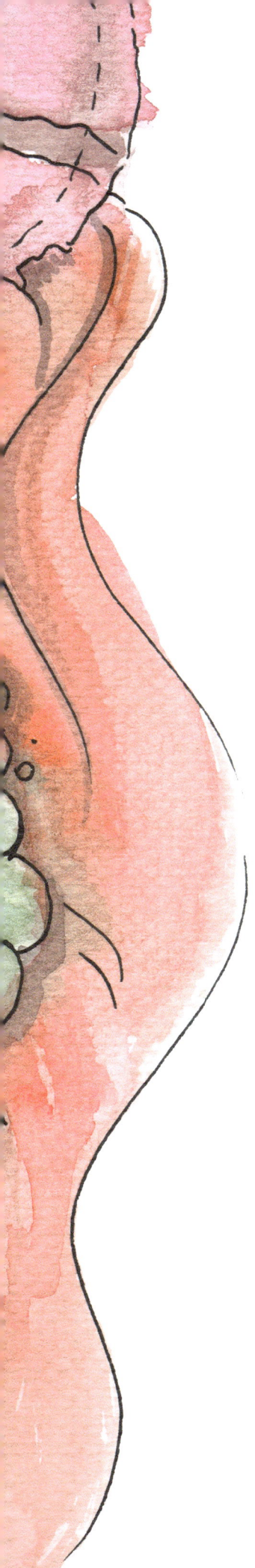

Although Rosie is asleep, her body is still working and Bertie soon finds there are new places for him to go. Sloshing around in this warm yellow pool he suddenly spies an opening to the right side of the stomach. This opening is known as a 'pyloric sphincter'.

Without warning Bertie is sent with a BIG...

through the pyloric sphincter, shooting into a new part of Rosie!

CHAPTER 3
The small intestine...

Bertie realises he is now in a tube in Rosie's body. This tube is known as the SMALL intestine. It has 3 parts – duodenum, jejunum and ileum.
The very l -o- n- g tube curls, loops and bends in order to fit into Rosie's little tummy. It is about 5 metres long, almost as tall as a giraffe.

He notices there are some tiny things that are carrying him along the tube. 'Who are you?' asks Bertie. 'We are called villi,' they all reply. Bertie chuckles. The villi work like very small fingers moving Bertie along as if he was on a wave. They guide him through the l-o-n-g tube by gently squeezing and cuddling him, making him into yet smaller pieces. 'Ohhh,' says Bertie, 'this feels lovely!'

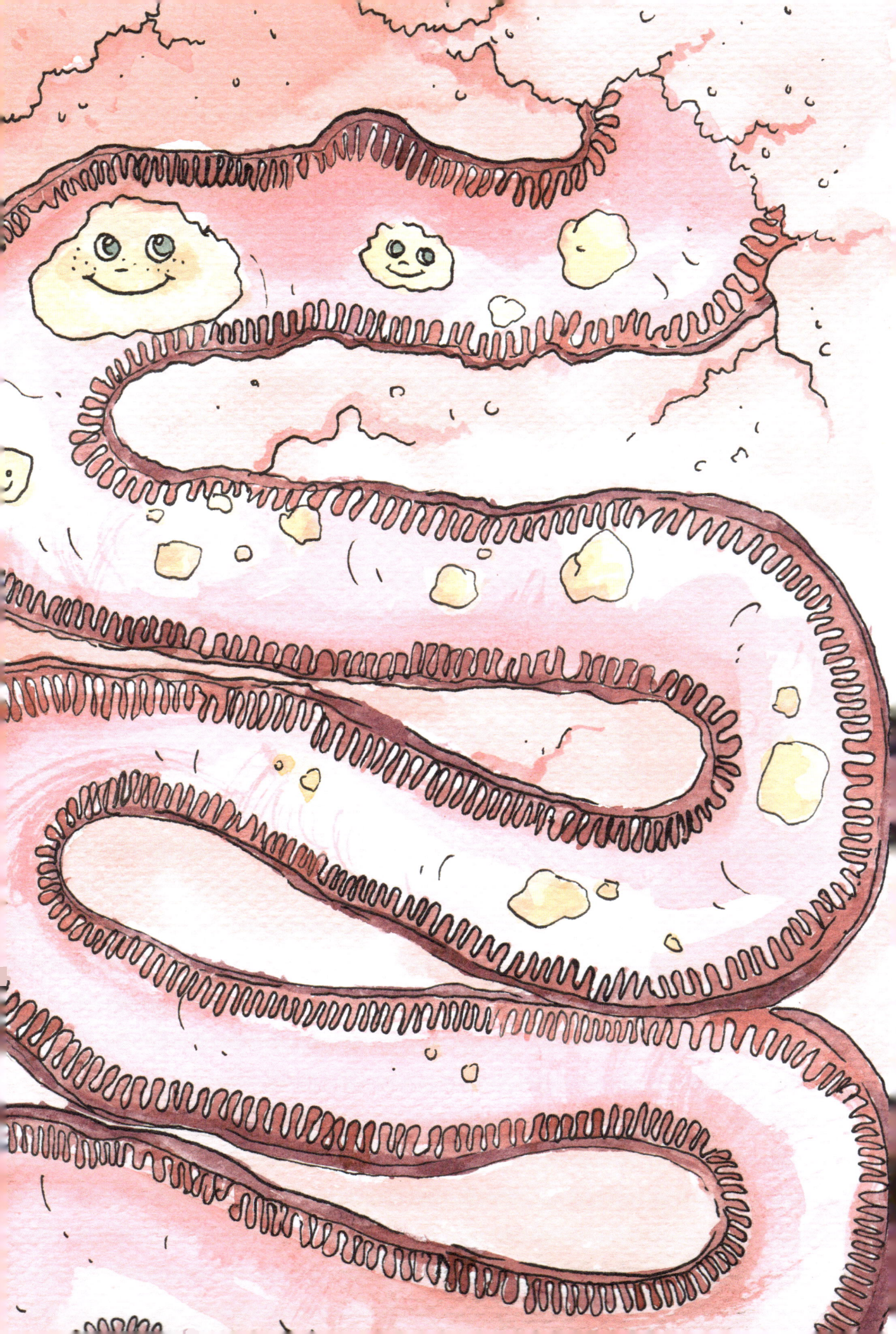

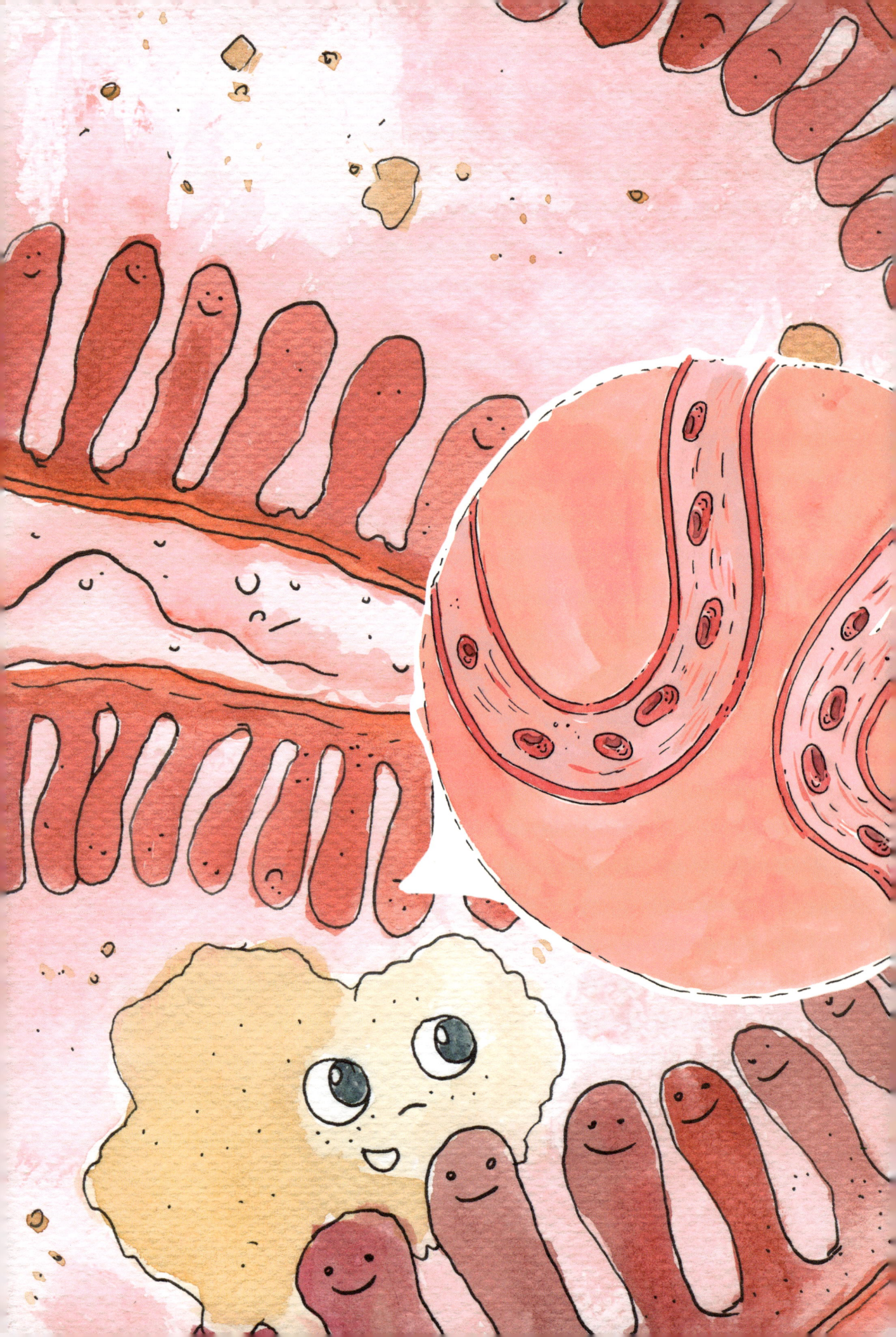

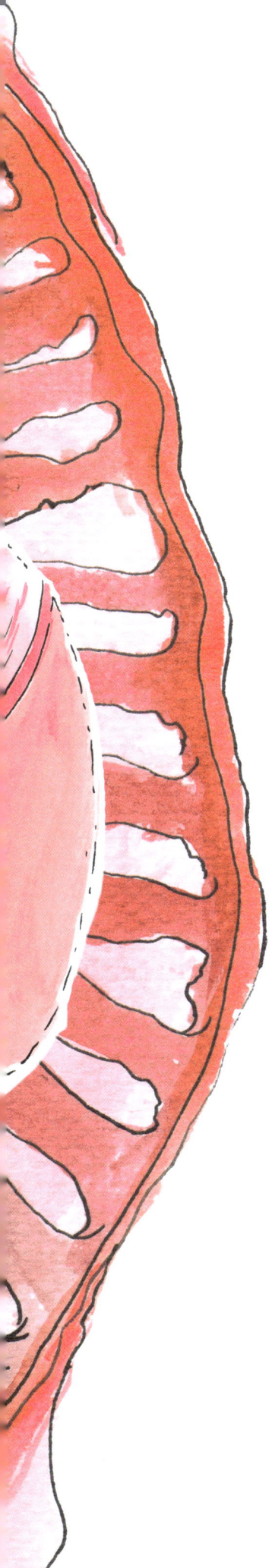

Rushing along through thin elastic tubes within the villi, Bertie notices some red liquid. This is something called blood – Brucey Blood! Through these tubes, known as blood vessels, Brucey flows like a river around the inside of Rosie's body night and day carrying important things from one part of her body to another. He is really friendly and asks: 'Please, can I have a few tiny pieces of you Bertie to take to other parts of Rosie's body?' Bertie was not too sure about this. 'I've already been made into smaller bits by that tube the 'Small Intestine' thanks. So no, you're not having any 'bits' of me!' he says, grumpily.

'That's a shame,' says Brucey. 'You see Bertie, you are made from some very important things like calcium which Rosie could use for her teeth to make them strong.' This makes Bertie giggle to think that he could become something as important as part of a tooth! Brucey is pleased this made Bertie giggle. So he continues: 'I can also take some of the calcium and give it to the BIG white things in Rosie body called bones. These bones stop Rosie's body from being all floppy. The calcium makes the bones grow l-o-n-g-e-r, making Rosie taller so that her clothes become too short!'

Brucey seems to be full of knowledge as he continues: 'You also contain other things Rosie can use Bertie like fats, vitamins, proteins and carbohydrates. They can be used for things like giving her lots of energy in her muscles so that she can run and play with her friends. If she doesn't have strong muscles she will feel weak, tired and will only want to sit around all day.'

'I can also use bits of you for Rosie's skin so that if she falls over and hurts her knee, the skin could then use these things to make it all better and stop me making too much of a mess!'

'OK, OK,' says Bertie grinning 'You can have the bits you want.' Being able to help Rosie with all these things makes Bertie feel very important and full of pride.

It is now mid-afternoon and the warm sunshine on Rosie's face has woken her and she decides to go outside and play with her friends. Even though Rosie is out playing, Brucey Blood is still really busy. Bertie cannot believe how much time Brucey spends coming and going taking special little bits from him.

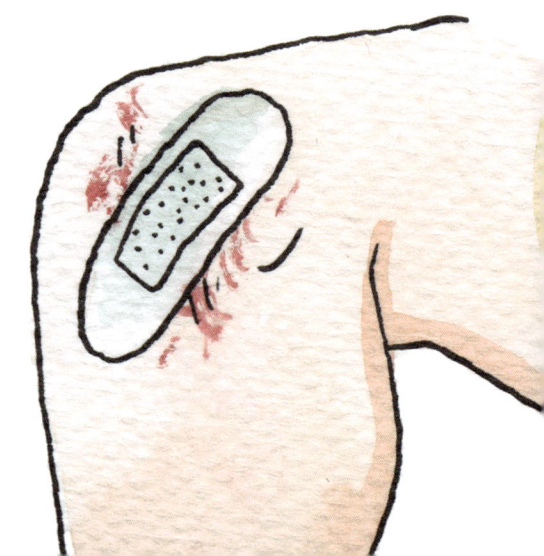

He suspects Brucey is taking much more than he originally promised, but Bertie doesn't mind as he knows it will be used to make Rosie happy and healthy. He just sits back and enjoys the ride in this little tube.

CHAPTER 4

The LARGE intestine...

5ft long...

Hours go by. Rosie comes back inside, has a meal with her Mum, and then goes off to bed. Bertie is near the end of the SMALL intestine and although he has enjoyed the gentle squeezing and cuddling and meeting Brucey Blood, he starts feeling tired and wants a rest. He is very happy when he enters a bigger tube...

This bigger tube is called the LARGE intestine. Most people call it this but some medical people call it the colon. It is about 1.5 metres long, which is as wide as a big bed. There is more room for Bertie here, no more squeezing and squashing! There is still movement but it is gentle and slower.

Bertie takes a look at himself and exclaims: 'Oh my goodness, there is hardly anything left of me!' In fact, when he takes a closer look he finds he is now only made up of a few stringy brown fibre pieces. They are mixed up with some green liquid known as bile that had been with him since he was in the small intestine. Oh, how unhappy this makes Bertie feel. He started the day feeling big and proud and all puffed up. Now, he is very tiny. Then he starts to think about what he has done to make Rosie BIG and STRONG.

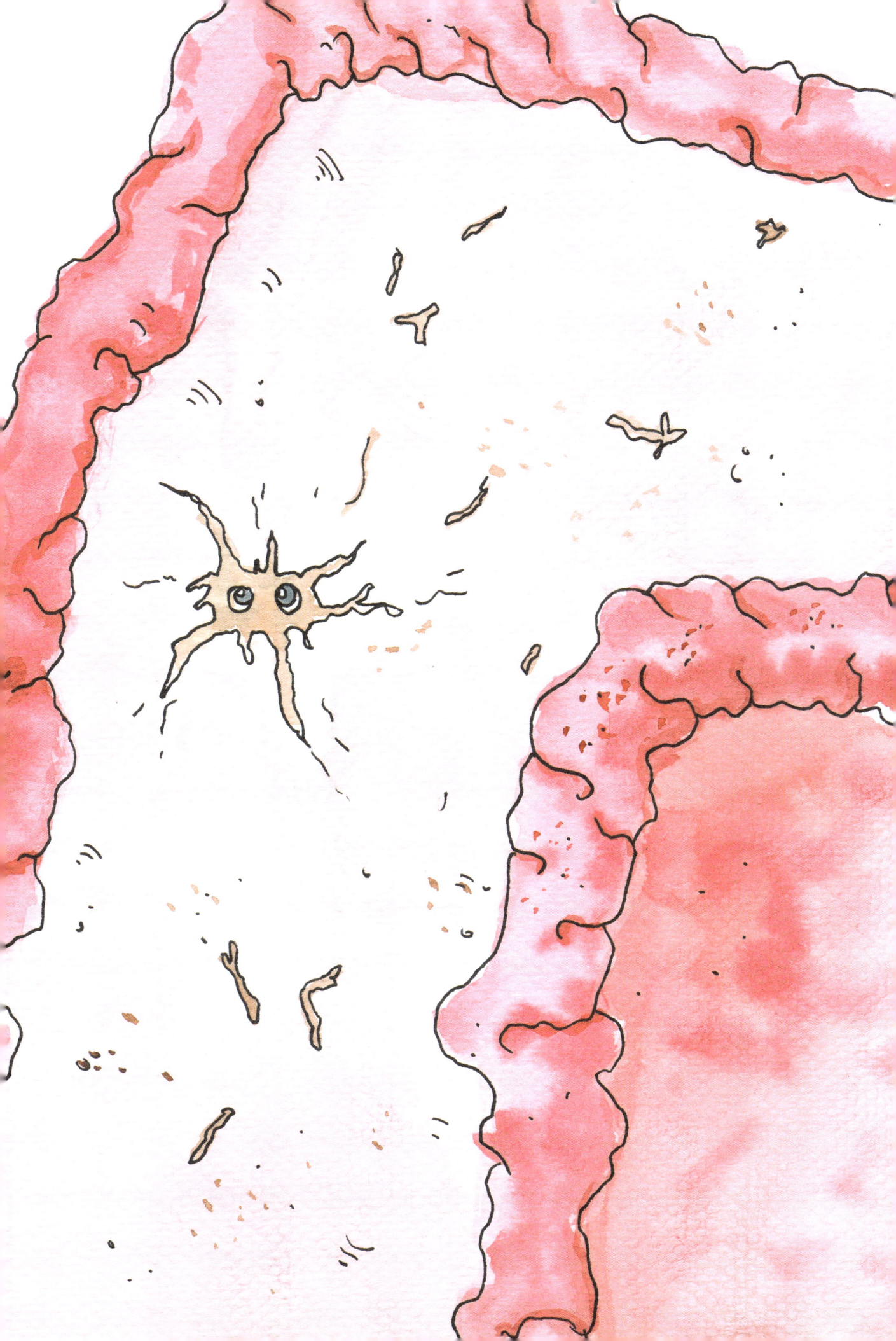

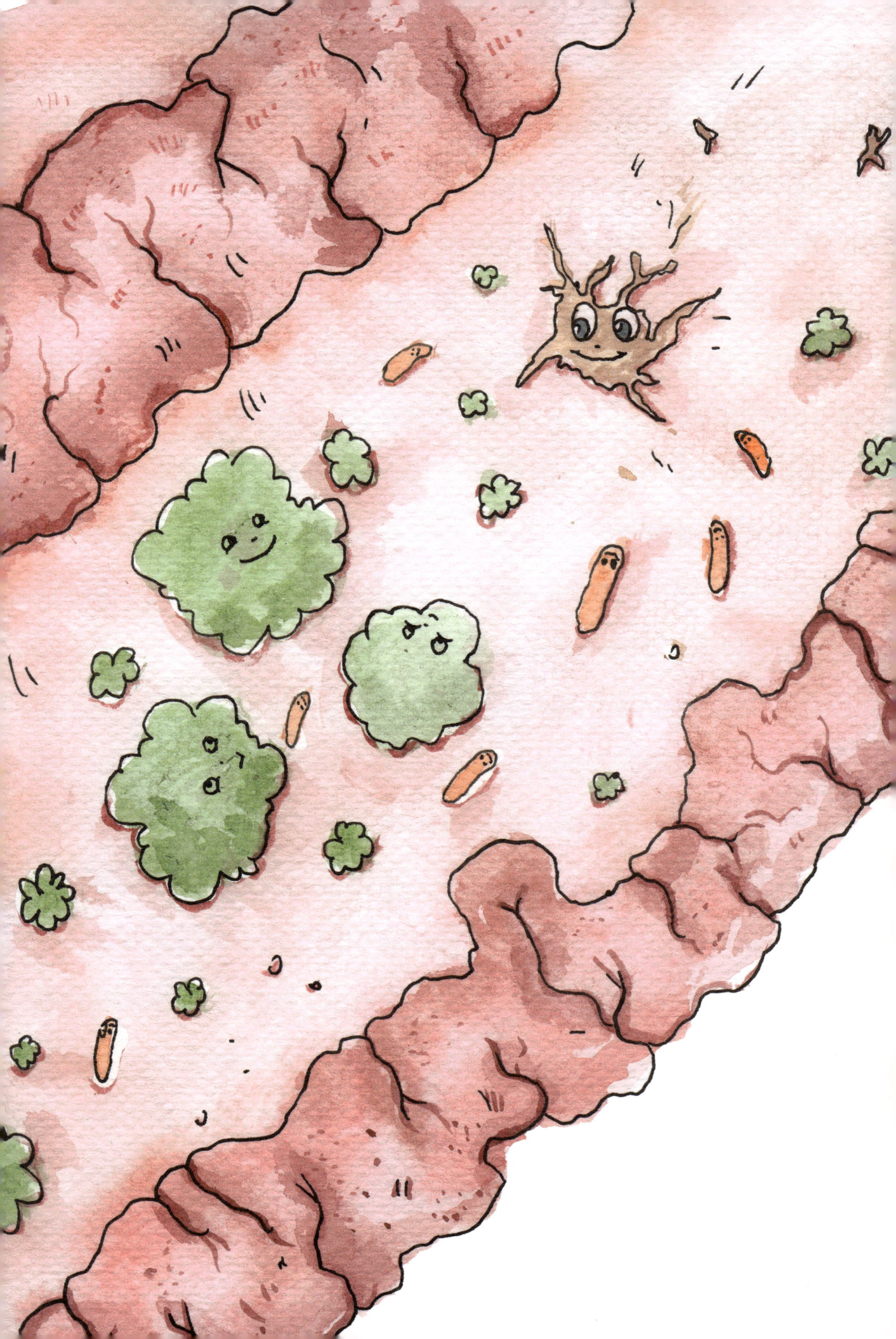

'Brucey has taken all my important bits,' he thinks to himself with a smile. 'He will have taken them to lots of places all over Rosie's body and some will stay there for quite a few days while Rosie plays and sleeps.' These thoughts stop Bertie feeling sad and instead he feels very pleased with himself.

The Gas Family are also in the LARGE intestine. They slowly joined Bertie all the way from the big yellow pool but Bertie has only just noticed them. They bubble and bobble along with him. They are gentle and kind but a bit noisy at times! More gas is being made by their friends called bacteria. Bacteria enjoy playing with food like Bertie in the LARGE intestine. They break the food up into smaller bits but in doing this they create even more bubbles. All night long, while Rosie sleeps, the Gas Family mix together with the bubbles made by bacteria in Rosie's tummy.

In the morning Rosie wakes up after a good night's sleep. All the time Rosie has been dreaming Bertie has been slowly moving down the LARGE intestine where the final bits of liquid have been removed from him. The stringy pieces left of Bertie, end up in a little soft round pocket at the end of the LARGE intestine. This is known as the rectum. When things fill this pocket you feel like using the toilet. This is exactly what Rosie feels like. The Gas Family and bacteria have been really busy which makes her tummy feel very windy. When she gets out of bed and stands up there is a big...

and a lot of wind comes out of her bottom!

Still sleepy eyed she goes to the bathroom and sits on the toilet. The soft pocket opens up and before you can shout...

the brown bits plop into the toilet. At the same time the Gas Family fly all over the bathroom. 'Pooh,' thinks Rosie, 'what a smell!' Although a few last bits of Bertie are in the toilet, most of him remains in many different parts of Rosie's body. As Rosie finishes, her mother calls: 'Rosie! Your breakfast is ready. Don't forget to wipe your bottom, pull the flush and wash your hands.'

I wonder what will be making its way through Rosie's digestive system today?

Where has Bertie been?

1 **Pharynx (far-rinks)**
Cavity at the back of the mouth.

2 **Oesophagus (ee-soff-a-gus)**

3 **Stomach**

4 **Pyloric Sphincter (Sfinkter)**

5 **Small Intestine (duodenum, jejunum, ilium)**

6 **Large Intestine (Colon)**

7 **Rectum**

Bertie in the yellow pool

Bertie with the Villi

What does it all mean?

Bacteria These are very small organisms that are all around us and on our skin. Some bacteria can cause disease. Most are harmless. Some, for example those that live in the intestine, are beneficial and help to break down the food during digestion.

Bile is digestive juice produced by the liver. It is a yellow-green colour, quite thick and is stored in the gallbladder until the body needs it. It helps to break down fats in the small intestine and also carries away waste products formed in the liver.

Blood is the red liquid that flows around the inside of your body and you can see it if you cut yourself. It flows like a river through tiny elastic tubes (known as vessels) around your body pumped along by the heart. It takes things like the air that we breathe and the food that we eat to different parts of the body to help keep us alive. It also plays an important role in protecting us against infection.

Calcium is soft and white. It is used for making strong bones and teeth. It is also used to keep the muscles healthy and is in the blood to help with clotting (for example forms the sticky lump you see when you cut yourself which stops you bleeding too much). It can be found in many things including milk, bread, eggs and vegetables.

Carbohydrate These are found in certain kinds of food such as sugar, cereals, bread, pasta and potatoes. It provides the body with energy. If you have more than you need for energy in your body, it is changed into fat.

Colon See under 'Large Intestine'.

Digest / Digestion is the process of food and fluids being moved from the throat to the rectum. The process breaks down food and makes it into things that the body can use; for example protein being used to make muscle.

Gastric Juices secreted from glands lining the stomach. It is used to break down food in the stomach and kill bacteria. It is the yellow stuff that comes up from your stomach sometimes if you vomit.

Fat one form is contained in foods such as meat, cheese, oil, butter and nuts. It contains important vitamins needed for the body to function. Fat is an important part of a healthy diet especially for little children as it is needed to develop the nervous system and brain correctly. It can be used for energy, to help keep you warm and to form body fat. Body fat lies beneath the skin and around some of the internal organs. Excess amounts of fat are stored under the skin in obesity.

Fibre is bits of plants or seeds that your body cannot digest. Most vegetables and fruits contain fibre. It is also found in foods like cereals and wholemeal bread. It is very important as it helps food pass through your body. It assists with problems like constipation and other gastric problems. It can also help prevent cancers and reduce cholesterol levels.

Intestine The tubes through which food passes from your stomach to the rectum. There is the small intestine and the large intestine.

Large Intestine is the shorter and second part of the intestine. It is made up of three parts - the caecum, colon, and rectum. It reabsorbs water, vitamins and salts (from the food that has already passed through the small intestine) into the blood stream. What is left is later passed as faeces ('poo') into the toilet.

Muscle There are three types:
1. Skeletal muscle is a piece of tissue inside your body which is connected to your bones by tendons and gives your body shape. You use these muscles to make your body move.
2. Smooth muscles are in the walls of internal organs for example the intestine (peristalsis action which moves the food along); blood vessels; and the bladder.
3. Cardiac muscle which helps keep the heart beating thousands of times a day.

Organism is a general term for an animal or plant, quite often so small that you cannot see it without using a microscope. Bacteria and viruses are disease-causing microorganisms.

Oesophagus is the part of your body that carries the food from the throat to the stomach. It is part of the digestive tract. Powerful actions of the muscles in the wall of the oesophagus propel food and liquids down towards the stomach for digestion.

Pharynx This is the part of the body that carries the food from the mouth to the oesophagus. It also plays an essential part in breathing and can change shape to help form speech sounds.

Protein is found in food and drink such as meat, eggs, milk, cereals and nuts. You need protein in order to grow and be healthy. It can also be used for heat and energy.

Pyloric Sphincter is the small ring of muscle around the opening at the bottom of the stomach. Its function is to control the movement of partially digested food into the small intestine.

Saliva is the liquid that forms in your mouth when you chew your food. It helps to break down the food; keeps the mouth moist; lubricates the food so that it is easier to swallow and helps the tongue and mouth to register taste.

Small Intestine is the first and longest part of the intestine. It is in 3 parts - the duodenum, jejunum, and ileum. Here bile and enzymes are mixed with the food to help break it up into tiny bits. This is where most of the important things in your food is digested and then taken (by the blood for example) to where it is needed in your body.

Stomach This is a bit like a sack and is between the oesophagus and the small intestine. Food is mixed together here with liquid known as gastric juices (the big yellow pool) and partly digested before it moves into the small intestine.

Villi are soft tiny finger-like things that are on the inside walls of the small intestine. They provide a large surface area for the absorption of tiny bits of food from the intestine into the blood stream.

Vitamins These are found naturally in a lot of foods and are also added to other things like breakfast cereals. They are really important, as the body will not work properly if it does not get enough vitamins every day.

Wholemeal flour is made from the complete grain of the wheat plant, including the outer part. It is much better for you than 'white' flour as it has more good things like vitamins and protein. It takes the body longer to digest and because of this you become hungry less quickly after eating it compared to 'white' flour.

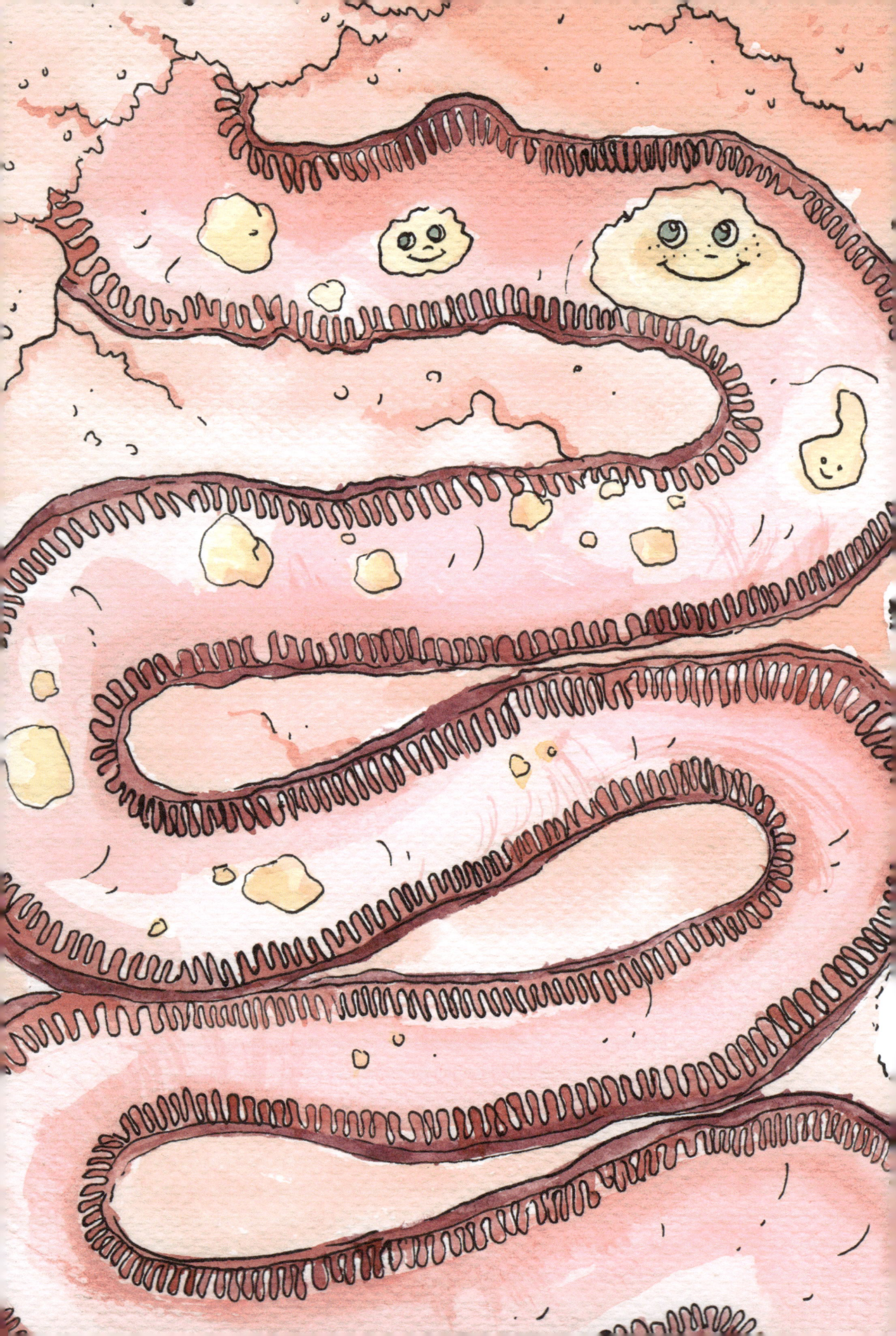

BERTIE BREAD WORDSEARCH

This word search can be photocopied as long as it is for educational purposes and related to the use of the Busy Body Series.

```
C X C K M I A P U X K K I P R
A C F P C S Y I V H M T G X S
R O B C G A X E R M O G G A V
B G Q A B N T X A E J T L Z I
O I N T E S T I N E T V A V L
H C A L C I U M X U I C V X L
Y X N Y R A H P L A L I A Y I
D O E S O P H A G U S S G B B
R E D I D R N W V M Z H Z L M
A Q L Q I V X N U M O O Z X A
T E R F K S S T G S B O H C D
E Y S T O M A C H C D J C V D
H D K K M R Y S A L U J I X I
O N B X X K A O Y E Y P G I J B
A A R E Z Q M V Y D E L I B D
```

BACTERIA
BILE
BLOOD
CALCIUM
CARBOHY-DRATE
INTESTINE
MUSCLE
OESOPHAGUS
PHARYNX
SALVIA
STOMACH
VILLI

Other Books by...

The Busy Body Series

Suitable for key stage 1 & 2
Written By Heather Hawley
Illustrated by Sarah-Leigh Wills

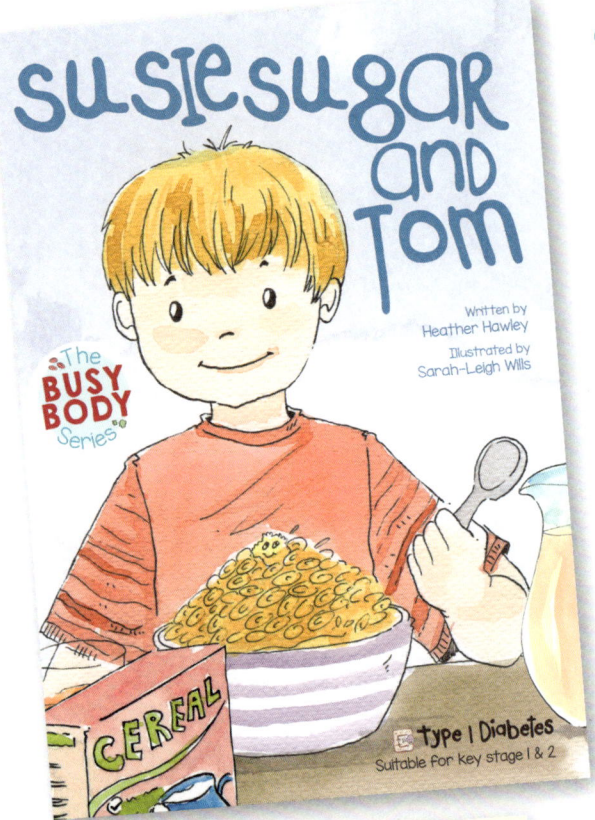

about...
Type 1 diabetes...

Susie Sugars adventures through Tom's body are used to explain the process of food being turned into glucose (then Susie Glucose!) and how the glucose is used for energy. She meets up with Brucey Blood who explains how insulin is needed to unlock the cells for Susie before she can be used by Tom for energy. Then they find that pancreas cannot produce any insulin and as a result Tom becomes ill. The story continues with Tom going to the surgery then the hospital for diagnosis and treatment of Type 1 Diabetes and finally back home.

ISBN 978-0-9931014-1-0

£6.99

about...
Kidneys and renal system....

The adventures of Josie Juice through Matthew's body are used to explain what happens to the fluid in our bodies. She meets up with Brucey Blood who explains how the water she is made of is important to Matthew. The journey starts as a glass of juice, which travels from the small intestine, through the renal artery to the kidneys, eventually being passed as urine. It even explains why Matthew ended up with a wet patch in his pants when he wanted to stay with his friends rather than go to the toilet!

ISBN 978-0-9931014-2-7

£6.99

The Author Heather...

"I have worked as an Advanced Nurse Practitioner (BSc (Hons) ACNP) in a GP surgery since 1999 and many of the patients I see are children. Working with children in the medical field can be challenging. Sometimes a creative imagination is useful in order to gain their confidence; this can help the children and their parents to understand the condition and the medical interventions we are making. With this in mind I decided to write the Busy Body Series."

The illustrator Sarah...

"My style of illustration has regularly been referred to as fun and inventive, the 'quirky designer' being a nickname I have regularly heard. My focus is now on childrens books, 98% of my work these days is just that, and I couldnt think of anything better, a complete excuse for me NOT to let my mind grow up!! I love creating educational books for children, in fact its now a passion of mine, helping them understand through my illustrations. ... and I LOVE music & Haribo!"

Find out more at: www.busybodyseries.co.uk